# Your Sign Is Down!

# Your Sign Is Down!

## SIX FEET UNDER

R.D. Zaragoza

**VANTAGE PRESS**
New York

*Cover design by Polly McQuillen*

FIRST EDITION

All rights reserved, including the right of
reproduction in whole or in part in any form.

Copyright © 2004 by R.D. Zaragoza

Published by Vantage Press, Inc.
419 Park Ave. South, New York, NY 10016

Manufactured in the United States of America
ISBN: 0-533-14854-5

Library of Congress Catalog Card No.: 2004090516

0 9 8 7 6 5 4 3 2 1

For my family and close friends who understand me

# Contents

| | |
|---|---|
| *Author's Notes* | xi |
| *Restless beings. . . .* | 1 |
| *Standing there . . .* | 1 |
| *They never come out at night. . . .* | 3 |
| *Eyes opened . . .* | 3 |
| Sleep Disorder—Self-Imposed | 5 |
| *I do not . . .* | 6 |
| *Respect for life. . . .* | 6 |
| *All that matters is you . . .* | 7 |
| *I have prejudice . . .* | 8 |
| *Shouting. . . .* | 9 |
| It Is Not Hate | 11 |
| *Names with no faces. . . .* | 12 |
| *I've lived there . . .* | 12 |
| *I live in . . .* | 13 |
| *Stop this! . . .* | 14 |
| *What right . . .* | 14 |
| *Obdurate . . .* | 15 |
| *Listen to the wind. . . .* | 16 |
| Guns in the Hands of Children | 17 |
| *Of nothing . . .* | 18 |
| *Can you . . .* | 18 |
| *We brush . . .* | 19 |
| *You are alone . . .* | 20 |
| *Change. . . .* | 20 |
| *In puberty . . .* | 21 |
| *One, two, . . .* | 21 |
| Having Babies | 23 |
| *Then live the pain . . .* | 24 |
| *Shadows cast in shadows, . . .* | 24 |
| *Opinions . . .* | 25 |

| | |
|---|---:|
| *Warmth, . . .* | 25 |
| *I am . . .* | 26 |
| *Warped mind . . .* | 27 |
| *Heavy. . . .* | 27 |
| A Touch of Cold | 29 |
| *What point . . .* | 30 |
| *I have wept . . .* | 30 |
| *Slipped down, . . .* | 31 |
| *Fight to live. . . .* | 32 |
| *There is a story . . .* | 32 |
| *Rain drops . . .* | 33 |
| Girls Just Hanging | 35 |
| *Expired. . . .* | 36 |
| *Sign language, . . .* | 36 |
| *You ain't nothing . . .* | 37 |
| *Random acts of violence, . . .* | 37 |
| *Delinquent deeds . . .* | 38 |
| *What is the attraction? . . .* | 39 |
| *Language . . .* | 40 |
| Another Language | 41 |
| *Go then. . . .* | 42 |
| *Bring it back, . . .* | 43 |
| *No rain, snow, . . .* | 43 |
| *You've become . . .* | 44 |
| *Working hard to be careful . . .* | 44 |
| *They work hard . . .* | 45 |
| *Today, I ask you . . .* | 46 |
| Selfishness to a Point | 48 |
| *You set fires . . .* | 49 |
| *The clock ticks and the innocent fall. . . .* | 50 |
| *You kill my street . . .* | 50 |
| *Two lives you lead. . . .* | 51 |
| *If there is love there, . . .* | 51 |
| *Like hypnosis, . . .* | 52 |
| *A flip you make, . . .* | 52 |
| Dual Lives | 54 |
| *Stop the police! . . .* | 55 |
| *Don't talk about my mama. . . .* | 55 |

| | |
|---|---|
| *Free? . . .* | 56 |
| *Lawyer . . .* | 57 |
| *Hands stretch, . . .* | 58 |
| *Open up like a flower. . . .* | 59 |
| | |
| *Epilogue* | 61 |

# Author's Notes

To feel what transpires in a given community, one must dwell in it. Take it for a time and embrace it. Only then can the feel of it penetrate the senses. No one can be entirely blind, deaf or indifferent to the surroundings.

Living in its heart, is an experience that reveals the warmth and cold that envelop it. There may be an unequal measure of each. The heat of it may be much more evident. Even still, its coldness weighs heavy because it is difficult to understand. It appears to be without reason.

Too many factors lie behind the choices made by some that cause a stir. Those, few in number when compared to the whole, make it ugly for the rest. They cast a shadow and create a draft that chills the bones.

One wonders how the beauty and warmth of a people cannot prevent or usher the unfriendly atmosphere away. Instead, it lingers and grips so tight that many pop out. They move away, forgetting the warmth and losing it as well.

Those little that do not falter to terrorize, are to blame.

# Your Sign Is Down!

Restless beings.
Those that
do not sleep,
for fear their own
darkness will
swallow them.

In shadows
they wander
going nowhere,
but disrupting
the quiet
of our streets.

We cannot
set a trap,
for they feel
their own
methods
in the night.

Their fall
will come
we know.
By themselves
they will fade,
and few will care.

\*   \*   \*

Standing there
on the cold,
dark corner,
pretending
you fear nothing.

But death lurks,
not far
with open arms
to greet you,
little brother.

You give another
in return for
your own.
For the moment
that works.

Still, you do
not sleep;
knowing it will
return and may catch
*you* unexpectedly.

    \*   \*   \*

Sleep then,
for soon
it will not come.

Times will
follow, where
you have no rest.

Your many
new friends
will not let you,

As the deeds
given you
keep growing.

           Their agenda
            will keep
         you on the move.

          And, you will
            lie awake
        counting your days.

             *   *   *


They never come out at night.
We do not allow it.

In their beds, they lay asleep
dreaming with angels.

This may be what parents think.
It may be what they feel.

But, late at night after lights go out,
they leave their warm cocoon.

Away to join the rest of their troop,
under the glower of the moon.


           Eyes opened
            to a life
           of trouble,
          pain and fear.

          They will not
          close to sleep.

There is no
time to rest
in a world
full of energy.

Too busy to
be in peace.

It is no gift
born into it,
through family
and friends.

The walls
give no escape.

At every turn
there is more
to do that
must get done.

There is no
slowing down.

But more to
come before
the heart
suddenly stops.

Left walking
upright, but dead.

## Sleep Disorder—Self-Imposed

A good night of sleep is important to our health and ability to function throughout the day. People who lose sleep are aware of this, as when they experience a physical and mental drain that accompanies the loss.

We need sleep to survive. It is vital for our mental, physical and emotional welfare. When we do not sleep, we miss the benefits it contributes to every moment of our day and every part of our life. Depriving ourselves of a good night's sleep does little for our performance, mood and health.

The problem with some of our youths is they think sleep is only a time when everything slows down or stops. They can hardly slow down then, because they do not want to miss anything. Too much may be happening when they should be asleep. Thus, the little they may sleep is restless.

If they sleep too little, they miss the important part of how sleep restores us, and the problems begin. The fatigue and tiredness they experience during the day may put them in a depressed or irritable mood. This heightens their anxiety as they receive pressure from their peers that other things are more important and sleep becomes secondary.

Continual sleepless nights can cause headaches, but even worse, changes their personality. They may not be aware of it and attribute the change to a phase of their age. They are hardly ever refreshed with rest and may instead feel confusion and severe grogginess upon wakening. They experience difficulty concentrating, memory lapses and intellectual deterioration.

I do not
hate you,
my brothers.
But, I like
not what
you do.
*Although
we have
not met.*
The pain
you inflict
on others
does not
diminish
your own.
*To live in
peace, you
do not let.*
Although
you refuse
to see it,
you bleed
much more
than we.
*Even still,
deeper your
grave you set.*

\*   \*   \*

Respect for life.
You seem
to have none.

In a world
of love
and you see
only hatred.

Why should
you, if
you are dead?

To a world
of color
where you
only have two.

Which at
times you
wear with pride.

At others,
you slither
about trying
in vain, to hide.

\*   \*   \*

All that matters is you
and yet, you do not.

No one comes before,
but whom you follow.

Standing not in your way
except, to block you.

And you cannot move,
unless they let you.

I have prejudice
I must work
through and release.
I am disturbed.
These children
choose to be in gangs.

They belong to
me as brothers,
and children, too.
Even victims
they follow,
terrorize, and kill.

Some of us,
parents and friends
will not admit it.
Though we
see the delinquent
behavior growing.

We opt to turn
away and cannot
stop the spread,
of anger that
multiplies in
hearts that need love.

Which may be
all that is left
to revive the spirit.
But, it takes
effort and each
day, I grow more tired.

It is their life
I think, and
Still, I agonize.

*   *   *

Shouting.
Too much of it.
We forget to speak
and ears close
to the sound
so harsh.
Stop it.

Pushing far,
but not moving.
Yet, close enough
to every edge
to drop and
hit bottom.
Hold it.

Weighing
down with
change, first free
then setting
down rules
a little late.
Lost it.

Creating
an empty heart
that has vanished
away from a
home, leaving
a void.
Fill it.

Escaping
one life to lead
another often filled
with things
even farther
from warmth
Save it.

## It Is Not Hate

Hate, like love, is a four-letter word. However, it is quite the opposite, and a harsh and lonely word with nary a friend, but those with whom it may be best not to associate.

It is a feeling that alienates one from another, creating a gulf left bare. It is like a crater that easily begins to fill with unpleasant things like garbage, because it will not remain vacant and love for some is not an option.

People use hate like a weapon or tool to rip apart rather than build. Many recognize this and still let the emotion take control of an aspect of their lives, if not all of it.

Often, however, the use of the word is incorrect when describing the expressed feelings toward another. The more appropriate word is indifferent. Because one cannot detest another, with whom he is unfamiliar. One can be unfeeling though, or empty of emotion.

This indifference, I believe, is what drives some people to create a wall between themselves and others. They may not, as with hate, feel and act openly hostile to others. Yet, their rigidity is what may cause some individuals to hurt others without a second thought.

One can say it is just as bad as hating. The behavior hardens the arteries. The heart is less lively and begins to feed off the body from the inside out. The mind follows it in cold precision and helps prepare the body for its grave.

Names with no faces.
Why do I cry?
They should not be there.
Carved on a wall.
Made of stone.
Dead.

Names to remember.
Why should I care?
This should not have been.
Better left unborn.
Now there is a
void.

Names with no form.
Why am I angry?
They no longer have life.
Entombed below.
Now turned to
dust.

\*   \*   \*

I've lived there
and know
what happens.

I am angry that
your youth
you waste away.

Your growth stifled,
choked young,
leaving only pain.

No one stands
with you
where you now lay.

      \*   \*   \*

I live in
their midst.
All I see
comes from this.

Cowards
they are
that shoot
from afar.

One on one
not at all,
do they enter
a brawl.

But, bullies
they be
when someone
lone they see.

Should alone
they try to defeat,
they would be
easily beat.

For they
are not brave,
obvious in the way
they behave.

      \*   \*   \*

          Stop this!
          Madness
          is all it is,
          and has
          no root.
          But now,
          is seen
          as our
          culture.

          \*   \*   \*

What right
have you
to trespass?
Entering
another's
property.

No good
will come
of doing so.
But, you
persist in
that path.

The fight
to stop
you, goes on.
And neither
they nor
you let up.

          \*   \*   \*

Obdurate
Obfuscate
Oblivious
Objection
Obnoxious
Obscene
Obscure
Obsecrate
Obsequy
Obsess
Obstacle
Obstruction
Obtrude
Obtund
Obtuse
Obvert
Obviate

Listen to the wind.

A sound in
the distance
that wakes.

The dead that walk.

I hear it bark
every night,
aggravated.

The dark shelters.

As they walk
by with sticks
and stones.

No one sees them.

But shadows
against the
wall forming.

Shapes of creatures.

In the light
of day they
are found dead.

But, the story continues.

More recruited
to replace
lives that were lost.

## Guns in the Hands of Children

Being unfamiliar with the ways of the street, at times on hearing of the violence, I am amazed and wonder how easy it must be to obtain a handgun illegally. I am later astonished at the age of those who handle them.

Why do they do it? Is it an initiation or just a warped mind acting violently? It must be both when it happens. Nevertheless, a child or youth firing a weapon in a free country is most certainly not normal. Yet, it happens too often in many neighborhoods where a small percentage of the youth run wild.

Wild, is perhaps a fitting word. For only an untamed heart can grip a gun and shoot at another without hesitation. An older individual might think twice or make certain the target is the intended.

Too many other factors come into play when it comes from the mind of a child. Reacting too quickly, acting without thought or upon command, fear someone will catch them and the repercussions, not caring, not knowing when or how to stop. All of these are reasons why youths and guns should not touch.

Of nothing
do they seem
to worry.

In the 'hood
with the rats
they scurry.

To the end
of their life
they hurry.

Only family
and friends
*may* be sorry.

\*  \*  \*

Can you
experience
love, when
you appear
to hate
humanity?

Then to you,
how can I?

Can another
show you
in return,
if you cannot
seem to do
so yourself?

Why then
should I?

\* \* \*

We brush
against it,
since it
stands close.

And lose
our breath,
but for
a moment.

Light, like
a feather
it dances
in our midst.

We invite it
not, but it
lives not far,
so is present.

It touches us
and still we
cannot get
used to it.

\* \* \*

You are alone
in this birth
you now hold.

The other
has run away,
to not own it.

Still, you must
continue on
with your life.

Find strength,
for the sake
of the child.


\*   \*   \*


Change.
You can
make it
happen.

If you
wanted
to, you
could.

Filter it
into
something
positive.

Give it
strength
and it would
blossom.

Instead
it wastes
away
your heart.

\* \* \*

In puberty
Introvert
In youth
Incorrigible
In disgust
Indifferent
In trouble
Inconsiderate
In pain
Intolerable
In agony
In crisis
In tears
Still a child.

One, two,
buckle my shoe.
Hung out all day with nothing to do.

Tick tack,
stubbed your toe.
Those silly games ended long ago.

Rock,
scissors, paper thin.
No longer care about who will win.

Red rover,
yell, red rover.
The children's play is finally over.

No one
plays—peek-a-boo.
Streets are empty, except for you.

Even if
things change each day,
there still are things you like to play.

Hit and run,
you love to tag.
You're the best, of that you brag.

Spin the bottle,
always meets your lips.
Litter on corners with used up clips.

Cover the eyes,
Hide-and-go-seek;
playing nasty on those who are weak.

Hush little baby,
don't say a word.
Someday you'll die, by your own sword.

# Having Babies

Four out of ten girls become pregnant in the United States at least once before age twenty. The number of teen pregnancies and births in this country is higher than any other country. Being first in this matter may not be something of which to be proud.

Every day, thousands of teenage girls learn they are pregnant. Teen pregnancy is a problem that affects nearly every community. We may behave unconcerned and believe it is not our crisis because we do not know the young girls who find themselves in this predicament. However, the responsibility to solve this problem lies with all of us, including families, communities, and young people themselves.

It is no easy task to solve, as it entails the willingness of youths to listen and understand the responsibility of having and raising a child. They must think long-term before taking any action and should recognize that sexual intercourse can lead to pregnancy.

Many youths can no longer use the excuse that they were unprepared because they were not planning to have sex. Too many organizations, including schools, teach sex education so teens understand how to avoid pregnancy.

These emphasize that all teens are entitled to opportunities to fulfill their potential. Many avenues for learning underline that teens should be concerned with good health, practice self-respect, become responsible decision-makers about sexuality, and realize that the choice can sometimes lead to being an unwed mother.

        Then live the pain
         if you so choose.
        No one can really
           stop you.

        Not pain you say,
        but a network
    of friends that stand
          together.

      On street corners
     looking for trouble
     and there it will
         find you.

      It happens to all
       who are with
    you. Thus, you feel
       it is right.

        \*   \*   \*

Shadows cast in shadows,
where you hide from what
you fear, but are fearless.

Brave-standing soul, alone.
Dancing eyes thrust beneath
a hooded jacket no one sees.

Beneath the layer of anger
lies a child on the edge of tears
brimming, but will not fall.

Reaching out with hands
stretched in pockets, to no one
willing to pull you back.

Opinions
I hold,
Some harsh.

I judge.

Not
Because I
Am better;

Merely,

Stricter
In discipline,
As I was
Reared.

\*   \*   \*

Warmth,
we all need
in spite of
the weather.

Cold emanates
from some,
causing us
to shiver.

They touch
us briefly,
but leave
a draft.

Like an
open door
in the dead
of winter.

\*　　\*　　\*


I am
as bad
as you are.

You do
not care
whom you hurt.

Anger
then starts
to boil within.

And I,
in turn
would hunt you.

To make
you pay
for what you've done.

How then,
do I
differ from you?

\* \* \*

Warped mind
bent from hits of
smoke and metal
from families
and friends
with no love.

Causing pain
that curls the body
out of shape
becoming yet
another
unrecognizable fetus.

\* \* \*

Heavy.
Heavy heart.
Heavy hearts, we cannot breathe.

But, coldness of my breath is felt
as it is cut
short.

Shortcuts.
You take cuts that
weigh you down and keep you there.

How can you not feel the weight?
Can you feel the weight?
Weight.

Wait.
Wait and you will,
feel the burden of what you do now.

Of which, you will no doubt, pay later.
At a cost you will soon
know.

No.
No mercy will be given
the consequences of your actions.

That take away from others what
You want and do not have;
Life.

Life.
Lifeless and unfeeling.
Close to death, you invite it to come.

When it does, I sense it is *we* who
will feel more pain in our
hearts.

## A Touch of Cold

Some people lose their enthusiasm for life. There is little or no laughter in their lives to cause their hearts to smile. Life is completely unfair, bleak. Thus, they develop a callus or quit it by turning their back on it because of something that may have occurred. They turn cold, without human warmth and emotion, and hardly anyone wants to be around them.

Things in life are, at times, not fair. They may make it hard to live and cause severe pain. They break and bruise, leaving their mark. Sometimes an incident may weaken a person, cause a setback for a while.

Being stuck there however, is a problem. It can lead to self-pity, which is very harmful. Self-pity disturbs us and once we have withdrawn we are hardly able to get out. Even if we choose to swim in it for a while, we have to gather strength and move on. We must find a way to live in happiness by concentrating on what we have left.

To continue in life, we need to let go of lost causes and free our minds and arms. We cannot possess new things when we are full of the old. We must not let ourselves become accustomed to unhappiness, simply because we are familiar with it. We must gather strength to steal away from its cold grip and make room for warmth.

It takes courage and is possible only with willingness and determination. It takes an equal measure of nerve as well to remain in the presence of one who casts a draft. Our instinct is to flee to avoid its touch. Perhaps a simple embrace would be sufficient to return warmth to those who are void of it.

What point
do you make
by hanging
ugly,
with people
who do
not care?

What once may
have been
your beauty,
is erased
and you are
left with
nothing.

Changed, though
you may want
to remain
the same.
And, perhaps
with a child
you do not want.

\*   \*   \*

I have wept
for the children
who have fallen,
victims to your
*evil* prey.

And *hardened*
my heart to the
so-called troubled
rearing you use
as an excuse.

You had chance
to fix it, but instead
chose to hurt those
who have done
*nothing* you.

\*   \*   \*

Slipped down,
into the cracks
of the ground.
Lost in the
concrete slabs
of sidewalk.

Flat stone.
Nothing can
penetrate.
Hardly disturbed
by the changes
in weather.

Yet, a collector
of garbage
left behind.
By those who
do not care
to sweep it.

But, walk all
over it with
no regard.
Not seeing what
they have
stepped upon.

      \*   \*   \*

Fight to live.
Find comfort with family.
With them, break bread.

They are the bond.

Not to die
carrying the heavy load,
of things that are dead.

      \*   \*   \*

There is a story
to the doll that lies
face down upon
a roof of a garage.
I can see it from
the train platform.

Rigid, stiff from
the diverse weather.
It has been beat,
pressed down and
now stuck. It cannot
move as once it did.

In arms that held it,
now it may no longer
be loved or cradled,
as it was cast aside
in anger or replaced
by something else.

From where I stand
I want to trespass,
climb the roof and
retrieve it. Free it.
Thinking I can
again give it life.

My mind reaches
out for it, feeling I
can still save it,
cleanse and redress it,
as its form is
still quite visible.

I know, even were
I to succeed in its
repair, its owner
would likely not want
it returned, as it was
already left for dead.

\* \* \*

Rain drops
to water
the earth.

I am visible,
he sees me,
where once
no one did.

A newfound
blossom I
have become.

I now have
someone
that gives
me his love.

What you see
now, is a
rose in bloom.

He takes me
and shares
me with all
of his friends.

My petals
scatter wildly
in the wind.

For to trust,
they must be
known to me,
and I to them.

And, I close
up to hide
the secrets.

## Girls Just Hanging

They lose their beauty. The wind, constant exposure to the outdoors, or just the lifestyle takes a toll on their good looks and they change. Many hardly realize it, do not care or actually think they are better for it. They may think they have grown and are more mature.

I often see young girls hanging on the corner in groups, sometimes even accompanied by boys, their counterparts. Sometimes, they look as if they are minding their business, just having fun. Other times, it seems, they are looking for trouble, what idleness does, and find it.

I wonder what the attraction is, if any. With so many opportunities in life, they chose a path that no doubt brings troubles. I question why they do it. Why do they spend their precious youth depleting it rapidly?

What I do know is, the problem is growing. They are out there, hanging on corners, in the parks, with bad boys and other bad girls. They are not all bad, or always bad. If they are, they must like it. They must be attracted to some aspect of a life that previously was merely boys being bad, which is bad enough.

They change to impress, to fit in. They go with the flow. In the process, they lose so much. My mother always said, "A woman loses more in any relationship." Could that be because they give more?

A hard life can waste you away. Looking for love in a lane that moves so fast, you have to do all you can to keep up. They might be children trying to escape reality and responsibility. Yet, they have to grow up quickly at times, left hanging with their own child.

Expired.
   You think it will
      not come to that,
         but all things end
            and not always good.
Expired.
   It happens around
      you, caused at times,
         by you. Yet, you
            feel immortal.
Expired.
   You cannot count
      the number of times
         you have visited graves
            or the dead in a parlor.
Expired.
   Others were caught
      off guard. Thus, do
         not be surprised
         if you are next.
   And
      Down
         You
            Go.

\*   \*   \*

Sign language,
a part of the rules.

Shoes untied
you cannot walk straight.

Tilt when you drive,
or your cap to the side,

Shoulders slouched,
colors must be kept right.

No hair on your head
nor a smile on your face.

Of who you once were
there remains no trace.

\* \* \*

You ain't nothing
but what you write
upon a wall.

Marked in spray.
No spelling correct
and all shaky.

'Cuz you can't
let them see you
tagging it up.

You've gotta make
a run for it before
you get caught!

\* \* \*

*Random acts of violence,*
*there is no such thing as peace.*

*All things seem to crumble,*
*when you are in their midst.*

*Perhaps you move about,*
*destroying things in your path.*

*Angry because they represent*
*what you'll never have.*

*Your life and all you touch,*
*soon turn from life to stone.*

*It will all soon fall apart,*
*and there, you'll stand alone.*

*You do not fully understand,*
*and thus, continue your guise.*

*Thinking it will be years*
*before someone your age dies.*


Delinquent Deeds
Often Oppressive Ones
Annoyed at Another's Advice

Dancing with Death in the Dark
Other Opportunities Overlooked
Adolescents in need of Assistance

Daily Determined to Damaging
Openly Odious and Offensive
Always Acting like Asses.

Do Not Disturb
Out of Order
Angry at All

Dangerous
Outrageous
Antagonists

Dead
On
Arrival

D
O
A

\* \* \*

What is the attraction?
   Do you know the answer?
      Are you bound to secrecy?
         Will I even understand?
           Does anyone really care?

Help me comprehend.
   Then you might too.
      See your hard edges from your fall.
        You need help removing the scab.
       For you are, still a youth.

Language
that says
nothing,
but sets
you apart
because
there is little
to understand.

You swear,
ugly sounds
that touch
ears, only
to push
you aside
as dense
when heard.

Yet cool,
you think
others feel
you are
after hearing
you rant
almost
incoherently.

Thus, you
continue
to talk in
words that
make many
cringe in
disgust in
your presence.

## Another Language

Hearing-impaired people learn sign language to communicate. It is a language using the hands and body to express oneself. Watching a person talking in sign language is intriguing because the movement is graceful, like a dance or bird in flight.

Others use sign language, however, that is not so refined. The movements are so brusque and ugly that we turn away from them. We want no part of that dialogue, whether or not we know it exists. We would much rather it did not, but often may be unsuccessful at preventing our children from learning it.

They learn from their exposure to it. It is present in certain areas they live or pass and strikes them, as does any sort of advertising.

Marketing and advertising are activities to attract others' interest. They are public announcements to proclaim the quality or advantage of something someone is trying to promote. They serve two purposes, to capture attention and to leave a mark.

We are living in what I call a "see me" world. The ones who shout the loudest, dress the barest, tightest or brightest, print the biggest and boldest messages get center stage. There simply may be no way to miss such exaggerations.

Some are entertaining, truly grasping and deliver a message worth receiving. Other times however, they become a nuisance. We are bothered especially when it is illegible rubbish printed on private personal property, which is the avenue used by delinquents.

Go then.
Dance in the street
with no hearth.
You will not find it,
though even
your home may be
***cold.***

You choose
by your own design,
to search for it
out in the open,
instead of
from that of your
***families.***

And still,
you are not happy,
evident in your
drawn face that
speaks clearly
of the pain you
***carry.***

Let it go,
free from the grip
of darkness that
filters through
clothing, words,
and signs the color of
***shadows.***

\*   \*   \*

Bring it back,
the peace once felt
on streets lined with trees
where you now hide.

You are not
lost and should
return from your cover
before no one seeks you.

\* \* \*

No rain, snow,
or blazing heat
keeps you away.

*A true love story.*

Hanging there
from dawn to dusk
without a care.

*At night, you return.*

As if distance
has made your
heart grow fonder.

*Or you have
nowhere else to go.*

\* \* \*

*You've become
like many
who think
"It's about me,"
which only
succeeds in
separating us
further.*

*Sadly, it never
really is
about you
as an individual,
but as part
of a group
that hardly
cares.*

*And, you are
lost amid
them, where
you remain with
your pain
hidden inside,
even you
cannot see it.*


Working hard to be careful
in the presence of police
and maybe even priests.

It is but a farce, as you heed
nothing of law and order
and likely have little faith.

Still, in their presence you
make every effort to say
what they may want to hear.

That they might leave you
on your own to continue
in your senseless behavior.

You hide your true self.
That way, you will not
create a bad impression.

In their midst, you pretend
you are innocent, as if
you turn the other cheek.

       \*   \*   \*

    They work hard
   to keep you straight,
   and still you bend.

   All they have done
   is merely for your
   family's own good.

   Blame them not
   for being simple and
   not what you intend.

   It is a poor excuse
   for you to use, for
   hanging in the 'hood.

Today, I ask you
just one thing,
to make you think
about your life.

See, what you
do, touches many,
although some,
you do not know.

Do you dance
happy where
you stand still
in the dark?

With friends
that come and go,
but hide from
life to live.

Afraid of shadows,
that are out at
night where
they waltz.

Not wanting to
yet, unable to
keep from
taking the step.

With every turn
you make not
looking to see
where you land.

Yet, we believe
each time you
know a part of you
on corners dies.

## Selfishness to a Point

"It's about me." At times, we make the mistake of being concerned only about ourselves. Songs and slogans emphasize it for us. We maintain that it is our life, our decision.

We forget our interconnection with others, or think we are quite singular. Thus, we can make decisions for ourselves, by our self. We go as far as thinking the choices we make cannot possibly affect another. How can they, especially if we are not concerned with their life and decisions?

This idea begins early on in our minds. We may disregard what our family or friends want and recommend for us, because we can think for ourselves. Then we think, if they do not support us in our choice, well, tough luck. We are going to do it anyway. Our thought becomes, "If they look out for themselves, then I must look out for myself."

We believe we are merely looking out for our own happiness. When we set out to do it then, we sometimes separate ourselves, particularly if others do not agree with us. If we do not get support, it becomes our own mission.

It is logical to think then, that if we fail, we have only ourselves to blame. This however, is not the case. We applaud our own successes, and attribute them to our own actions. However, failures are a result of our past and relationship with others. Here we share. We discount our behavior and downplay our self-involvement. The blame for our setback is due to others.

You set fires
to burn
things
or people.

Charred cars
along
streets
or alleys.

Crumbled
garages
blackened
with soot.

Smoke still
oozing
from some
of these.

Your fingers
itching
to keep
up the stroke.

Of matches
in your
pockets
ready to ruin.

\* \* \*

The clock ticks and the innocent fall.
By your hand, you do not build.
It is but a prank you think to pull,
to no avail on those you touch.
It will end. The hands will stop.
Time runs out and you with it.

\* \* \*

You kill my street
while trying for my spirit.
*That* you will not reach.

I will not die your death,
but will stand what I can
and move on if I must.

Then you will remain,
alone in streets strewn
with dirt and desolation.

Neither of us escapes,
but for reasons that differ.
I refuse to be pressured.

You however, are frozen
in time and to your spot,
because others rule you.

\* \* \*

Two lives you lead.
Yet, you are
not old enough
to live one.

That which you have
experienced,
you should wish
upon no other.

Still, you give them
no warning
of all the ugliness
you have seen.

Instead, you invite
others to join
in what can only
be called, misery.

\* \* \*


If there is love there,
let it begin and end
this drama of yours
before you cannot,
and become too ugly
to escape any harm
from those who make
you feel accepted,
but are nothing to them,
as they will not hesitate
to pull the plug, if
things go in disarray.
Do not let love die.
But, nourish it, as it
is all that can keep
from widening the

gap that now exists
between us and keeps
us from reaching one
another and coming
together in an embrace.

   \* &ast; &ast;

Like hypnosis,
it holds you
in a firm grip.
And, you do
not know, so
cannot work
to release it.

It grasps tight,
stopping your
circulation.
You breathe
less, almost
die, but yell,
don't let go.

A flip you make,
like turning a card
without knowing
what lies waiting
on the other side,
or how you'll fall.
Will it be a spade?

Because you will,
sooner than your
time, as you rush
to meet the end
of your life with
arms outstretched.
Or, perhaps a club.

Reaching to call
friends to follow,
that you might
not be alone on
corners, wasting
yourself to nothing.
Maybe a heart.

With thrashing,
wild arms in every
direction you drown,
in your efforts to
hold onto something
with open arms.
Cut on a diamond.

Where they remain
in anticipation, as
the dark will not
pass you like other
things, you could not
keep in your grasp.
Joker in the deck.

# Dual Lives

There are times many of us may wish we had a clone, so we could be in two places at once. Were that the case, we believe we could accomplish so much more than what we do ordinarily. It would be a luxury.

I jokingly tell family and friends that I wish I had one. Some agree with me. Others give me a look that leads me to imagine their thought process might be, "One of you is quite enough."

Having a duplicate to help chug along with life's responsibilities is somewhat different than living two lives. When we live two lives, or attempt to do so, we may run ourselves ragged. The two lives we try to lead may not converge. Thus, instead of making us whole, well-rounded individuals, our two lives give us split personalities.

That can happen throughout life but may be more prominent when we are in our teens. During those years, we are "trying to find ourselves" so we have our feet in many doors, constantly pivoting as we move from one to the other. Sometimes, we try to "far remove" ourselves from things that become unpleasant to us, but may not be entirely successful. Our foot catches or we stub our toe.

We make choices, move too fast, or slow, and are set back or trapped in a situation with no visible way out. This of course, is no fault of our own, as we do not often assume responsibility for our mistakes. Instead, we blame others and hide under that blanket of our supposed 'age of innocence.' With everything we encounter these days, that actual stage of our lives is shorter.

Stop the police!
They disturb
my child.

Mine has done
no wrong!

They dare to
take and put
him away.

What do they
say he's done?

Who was
there to
see this crime?

It must have
been the others.

For mine
knows better
and has no fault.

You accuse an
innocent child.

\*   \*   \*

Don't talk about my mama.
She's like a saint you see.

Though, I hardly treat her kind,
she's still the world to me.

I warn you just this once.
Don't put me to the test.

If you continue to disrespect,
I'll lay you down to rest.

\*   \*   \*

*Free?*

You are
not here
nor there.

*You believe.*

Other
than in
yourself.

*You escape.*

Chained
with whom
you hang.

*You wander.*

Trapped
to a set
of new rules.

*You follow.*

Never a
mind of
your own.

*You fear.*

By no
means then,
are you

**FREE!**

\* \* \*

Lawyer
Doctor
Dentist
Priest

See, this is
what he
meant to be.

Studying
Reading
Writing
Work

In all these
things, his
time he spent.

Gentle
Loving
Tender
Dear

A hand, he'd
lend to
all in need.

Brother
Friend
Father
Son

A true soul
of a saint,
now has gone.

\*   \*   \*

Hands stretch,
searching for another
where no one
wants to touch.

No warmth
then, reaches the
heart that soon
begins to close.

Like a disease
with no cure fast
enough, to kill
the pain within.

It seeps out
and others see it,
though you may
hide your face.

Eyes cast down,
so the body in turn
yells to the world
your misery.

\*   \*   \*

Open up like a flower.

Let the petals

fly to the wind.

Show the world,

beneath the thorns,

lies a rose.

# Epilogue

Unless you have lived there, experienced it, you cannot know. It is a war within a free country and does not make sense. It is a closed box within a very large open one, with so many opportunities.

They are free to choose, but choose wrong, because in their confines, they have little choice, or so they think. Much is lost when they go wayward, though they may seem insignificant. There are truly not very many, but enough to cause grief even to those who would rather remain at arm's length or better yet, further.

Not all is lost. Those who see beyond the boundaries, those who retain hope of an eventual escape, try to stand firm. That however, is no easy task. Sometimes they have little support. They cannot do it alone. If they try, the strength they have may drain, sucked out of them like blood by a vampire.

They are like diamonds in the mud, but these soon begin to lose their luster when the dust flies. A misstep by another could press them into the dirt and hide them. When this happens, it is crucial for others to intervene. Someone or others must care, seek them out, unbury them, and wash away the dirt. If they are not, they will remain lost because eventually they will look like debris. They will be confused for broken glass like their spirits.

Our indifference may add to the prospect of them never being found. Mostly, however, their descent is a result of being stepped upon by those who have lost or have never possessed hope before them. These too may be few in number, but their anger, wrath and misery leave little room for love. This lifestyle is their wealth, which they willingly share by seeking others to join them in their ugly loneliness. Their hatred is their force. It is a weapon used to repress and bully other more vulnerable beings.

They do it deviously, fooling and manipulating their victims. They show no mercy, which is not surprising, because if they do not even love themselves, they likely cannot love another.